TWO BOBBIES

A TRUE STORY OF HURRICANE KATRINA, FRIENDSHIP, AND SURVIVAL

Kirby Larson AND
Mary Nethery

ILLUSTRATED BY
Jean Cassels

Walker & Company 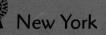 New York

*For all the pet rescue volunteers from across the United States
who lovingly gave of their time and resources after Hurricane Katrina,
and especially the good folks at Best Friends Animal Society*
—M. N. and K. L.

*To the New Orleans that is being built
day by day with love and determination by her citizens and visitors;
and to Annie, Rosie, and Chicory, who weren't left behind*
—J. C.

Text copyright © 2008 by Kirby Larson and Mary Nethery
Illustrations copyright © 2008 by Jean Cassels

First published in the United States of America in 2008 by Walker Publishing Company, Inc.
Distributed to the trade by Macmillan

Photograph on p. 32 courtesy of Barb Davis, volunteer with Best Friends Animal Society

For information about permission to reproduce selections from this book, write to
Permissions, Walker & Company, 175 Fifth Avenue, New York, New York 10010

Library of Congress Cataloging-in-Publication Data
Larson, Kirby.
Two Bobbies : a true story of Hurricane Katrina, friendship, and survival /
Kirby Larson and Mary Nethery ; illustrations by Jean Cassels.
p.   cm.
ISBN-13: 978-0-8027-9754-4 • ISBN-10: 0-8027-9754-7 (hardcover)
ISBN-13: 978-0-8027-9755-1 • ISBN-10: 0-8027-9755-5 (reinforced)
1. Dogs—Anecdotes—Juvenile literature. 2. Cats—Anecdotes—Juvenile literature.
3. Hurricane Katrina, 2005—Anecdotes—Juvenile literature.
I. Nethery, Mary. II. Cassels, Jean. III. Title.
SF426.5.L37 2008   636.08′32—dc22   2007049131

Typeset in ITC Highlander Book
Art created with gouache on 140 lb Arches hot press watercolor paper

Visit Walker & Company's Web site at www.walkeryoungreaders.com

Printed in Malaysia
2 4 6 8 10 9 7 5 3 1 (hardcover)
2 4 6 8 10 9 7 5 3 1 (reinforced)

All papers used by Walker & Company are natural, recyclable products
made from wood grown in well-managed forests. The manufacturing processes
conform to the environmental regulations of the country of origin.

Neither Bobbi the dog nor Bob Cat has a tail, and some say that's what brought them together. No one knows for sure how they met. Perhaps their owner had a soft spot for pets with no tails. But the Two Bobbies, as they've now come to be known, were each exactly the friend the other needed at exactly the right time.

This is their story.

The city of New Orleans, on the mighty Mississippi, is a place many people and pets call home. Jamming with jazz and dressing up fancy for Mardi Gras, it bustled with life day and night.

But on August 29, 2005, Hurricane Katrina bore down on the city and everyone who lived there, including a wisp of a cat and one puppy.

Winds roared to 110 miles an hour. Rain pounded hard and fast. Strong winds pushed walls of water from the Gulf of Mexico into Lake Pontchartrain. Some of the levees holding back the lake gave way.

Water poured into the city, deeper and deeper. People who had stayed through the storm were finally forced to leave their homes. They had to say good-bye to everything they loved. Many were told they could not take their pets.

Bobbi and Bob Cat were left behind. Bobbi had been tethered with a length of chain. Bob Cat stayed by her side. Together, in the silent heat, they waited for help to come.

After the storm, volunteers from across the country came to New Orleans to lend a hand. They brought food and water. They rescued people stranded on the roofs of their homes, and they rescued many animals.

But with so much damage and confusion, the Two Bobbies were not rescued. Their food and water gone, Bobbi finally broke free. She dragged along the broken chain with Bob Cat close beside her.

In the early days after the hurricane, the Two Bobbies tried to make their way around oily water littered with debris. After the waters receded, they traveled the buckled streets, with no place to call home.

Month after month passed as Bobbi and Bob Cat wandered the devastated city. Their days and nights were filled with danger. Packs of hungry, homeless dogs roamed the streets, fighting smaller animals for food. Were Bobbi and Bob Cat chased away from any scraps they might have found? With little food to eat or clean water to drink, Bobbi's ribs began to show. Bob Cat's brown-sugar markings started to fade to a dull white.

One day in January, four long months later, Bobbi
and Bob Cat strayed onto a job site. A construction crew
hammered and sawed, fixing up a motel damaged by the
hurricane. A worker's dog rushed over to play with Bobbi.
The dog's owner, Rich, noticed Bob Cat too. He saw how
thin the two strays were and began feeding them.

He trimmed Bobbi's chain, leaving enough to jingle on
the ground because Bob Cat liked to follow it. But every
time Rich tried to touch Bob Cat, Bobbi growled.

After a week of caring for the Two Bobbies, Rich got
some bad news when his boss came to the job site. He
had given permission for one dog—but not two dogs and
a cat. He said Bobbi and Bob Cat had to go.

Rich was determined to take them to a safe place. But Bobbi still growled whenever Rich got too near Bob Cat. She would not let him pick up or even touch her friend. So, Rich rattled a bowlful of kibble. Bobbi followed the food to Rich's van and Bob Cat followed Bobbi.

Rich drove them to a temporary shelter that Best Friends Animal Society had set up in Celebration Station, a former video-game arcade. The shelter was completely filled with homeless dogs and cats, but a volunteer welcomed them in, even naming them Bobbi and Bob Cat for their bobbed tails. They were placed in separate rooms.

All night long Bobbi howled and barked. Bob Cat paced back and forth.

No one could sleep with Bobbi making such a ruckus. So volunteers made a large pen for her and put Bob Cat, in his small carrier, inside Bobbi's new cage.

Bobbi lay in front of Bob Cat and whimpered.

The volunteers opened the small cage to see what would happen.

The Two Bobbies touched noses. Together again at last!

For the next few minutes, the volunteers studied Bobbi and Bob Cat. They noticed how Bob Cat stayed close to Bobbi. They saw how he walked with his neck stuck out and how he carefully lifted his front paws, placing them down as if he were unsure of what he might step on.

Someone waved a hand in front of Bob Cat's face. Bob Cat did not jump back. Another volunteer waved her hand. Bob Cat did not even blink. Everyone was stunned.

Bob Cat was blind!
All that time on their own, Bobbi had been Bob Cat's seeing-eye dog.

The volunteers, and even an ace pet detective, searched for their family—with no success. One month later, Celebration Station closed its doors. But Bobbi and Bob Cat still did not have a home. There was only one thing left to try.

The Two Bobbies
made a television
appearance on CNN's
Anderson Cooper 360°!

The very next day, the Best Friends volunteers left
New Orleans. One of them drove Bobbi and Bob Cat to
the Best Friends Animal Sanctuary in Utah, where they
would stay until a new family could be found. They were
on their way west when the news came in.

Hundreds of people wanted to adopt them!

It would take a very special family to adopt them together. The volunteers made a list and invited everyone on it to come and meet the Two Bobbies.

Only Melinda and her Boston Terrier Gus-Gus made the long trip to Utah. That night, Bobbi and Bob Cat had a sleepover with Melinda and Gus-Gus in one of the cottages on the sanctuary grounds. Would the Two Bobbies choose Melinda?

The next morning everyone knew the answer.
Bobbi and Bob Cat were stuck to Melinda like
Velcro. They also liked Gus-Gus, and he liked them.
Finally, Bobbi and Bob Cat had found their
new family.

Now they live with Melinda, Gus-Gus, and Amelia on a ranch in southern Oregon. Bob Cat has a window seat to sit in. He likes to play with the robot vacuum cleaner. He turns it on all by himself. Bobbi helps with the ranch chores. She goes along on horse rides. On hot days, she lounges in the frog and fairy pond.

At the end of every day, Bobbi and Bob Cat snuggle up together. They have toys and treats and lots of new friends—even a camel.

Best of all, they have each other.

After the Storm

Like thousands of others, the Two Bobbies lost their family and everything dear to them when Hurricane Katrina hit New Orleans. After they came to live with Melinda and Gus-Gus, their veterinarian discovered debris and grit deep inside Bob Cat's ear canals. His right eardrum was broken. Did Bobbi snatch Bob Cat from the dirty floodwaters that had filled New Orleans? No one will ever know. But it is very likely that a blind cat like Bob Cat would not have made it without Bobbi's protection. In turn, Bob Cat's friendship may have made Bobbi stronger and given her a reason to go on.

Bobbi and Bob Cat survived Hurricane Katrina.

They did it by lending each other a paw.

Bobbi and Bob Cat at Celebration Station